D1503656

Treasures
for Teachers

Treasures
for Teachers

Janet Colsher Teitsort

BAKER
A DIVISION OF
Baker Book House Co

© 1994 by Janet Colsher Teitsort

Published by Baker Books
a division of Baker Book House Company
P.O. Box 6287, Grand Rapids, MI 49516-6287

Second printing, September 1995

Printed in the United States of America

Library of Congress Cataloging-in-Publication Data

Teitsort, Janet Colsher.
     Treasures for teachers / Janet Colsher Teitsort.
        p.   cm.
     ISBN 0-8010-8917-4
     1. Teachers—Prayer-books and devotions. 2. Christian life.
  I. Title.
  BV4596.T43T45 1994
  242'.68—dc20
                                         94-16001

Dedicated to the
glory of **God**
and
to my mother,
Dorothy Black Colsher,
the first teacher
of my heart

Janet Teitsort teaches first grade at South Decatur Elementary, near Westport, Indiana. She is the author of *Rainbows for Teachers* and *Quiet Times: Meditations for a Busy Woman*. Her writings have appeared in such publications as *The Secret Place*, *Mature Living*, *The Church Musician*, and Day Spring greeting cards.

ontents

2 Jewels of Promise

3 A Treasury of Moments

# reface

If the hand that rocks the cradle rules the world, then the person who teaches can change the world. Teachers have a tremendous opportunity to help reshape the value system of our land. We have been gifted with the creativity to help solve the problems that arise when changes occur in society. Daily our students read our lives as if we were books. Often they learn more by our actions than by our words.

Writing this book has strengthened my faith. I have a new confidence in regard to my teaching. There are solutions for the problems that we must contend with. As we draw near to the heart of God and seek his wisdom, he is faithful.

It is my desire that this book will spark renewed hope within the hearts of teachers. May we teach with boldness, as we realize that we don't have to do it alone. The Lord Jesus Christ sees our needs and longs to help us, if we will turn to him.

At the end of each section are "My Treasures to Remember" journaling pages. As you record your treasures, may you become increasingly aware of how God has enriched your life through your students and your teaching.

To everyone who has gone the extra mile to assist with this work, I express my deepest thanks. Without your prayers and encouragement, I would have had a hard time keeping on. I know how precious your time is and that makes me appreciate you even more. May God reward you with his rich blessings.

PART ONE

Set in Silver

An idea well-expressed is like a de in silver.

Those who love and follow me are indeed wealthy. I fill their treasuries.

Proverbs 8:21 TLB

My Treasures

A child's smile,
a warm hug,
a parent's thank you,

A scrawled *I love you,*
a lesson well taught,
growth in a student,

More dear to my heart
than riches en masse,
these are my treasures.

They are my
pearls of great worth,
my precious jewels,
the silver and gold
of my emotions,
the *why* of my teaching.

Father, thank you
for enriching my
life with your children
and filling my treasury.

To every thing there is a season, and a time to
every purpose under the heaven.

Ecclesiastes 3:1 KJV

A School Teacher's Lament

Handing me my
change, the clerk
asks, "Ready for
school? It's only
two weeks away."
*They start asking
this in June.*

Smiling, I mumble
"Sure." I've learned
to reply in the
affirmative, for that
is what people expect.
*Teachers are supposed
to breathe, eat, sleep,
and love school.*

I do, but today
I long to tuck
summer away,
filing it within my

mind, keeping it
for a winter retreat.

Then when the demands
of the school year clamor,
destroying my tranquillity,
I would recall the
laid-back sounds of summer,
    the coo of the morning dove,
    the chirping of the crickets,
    the whisper of the cornstalks
    rustling in the morning breeze,
and my spirit would be soothed.

But the medley of greens,
singing shades of summer
will soon give way to the
hosannaing of the autumn leaves.
    Change is inevitable.
    School must start.

In the barrenness of winter,
I will be glad for the shelter
of bricks and mortar,
asphalt and concrete,
and a life-work
filled with purpose.

My spirit will be warmed
by the sunny hearts

of my students and
friends at school.

But next week will be
time enough for my
ode to summer. Today,
in my favorite season,
let me drink in the beauty
of milky white clouds
carressing a blue satin sky
and sunlight tap-dancing
on water to the tune
of its gentle lapping.

Father, help me to store
up these rich memories
of summer and thank you
for the golden days of
my summer vacation.

The Lord is still in his holy temple; he still rules from heaven. He closely watches everything that happens here on earth.

Psalm 11:4 TLB

Trusting His Wisdom

Names typed on
crisp white paper
conjure up images
of unknown personalities.

It is a new school
year and I hold within
my hands my new
class list.

Anxiously, I contemplate
my new students.
*Do I know
any of them?
How will they
rank academically?*

Already I am projecting
the coming year.
She'll be a good
student. I know
her parents. They'll
work with her.
Um, I've heard
of that one. He's
a real terror. He's
sure to make my
year difficult.

On down the list
I go speculating
about a year
that is still unscathed.

Father, help me to
stop this nonsense.
Instead, let me remember
you are in control.
You are aware of
every name on my list
and have allowed
each one for a reason.
Maybe the diligent to bless me
and the problems to teach me,
or because you think
I can handle them.

Whatever the reasons,
I choose to trust
your wisdom.
Fill me with eagerness
to meet my new charges.
Quickly form the bond
uniting us in a
year of togetherness,
a year to be treasured.

For now we see in a mirror dimly, but then face to face. Now I know in part; then I shall understand fully.

1 Corinthians 13:12 RSV

A Special Remembrance

It is time to start the
school year and the
teachers are bustling
with creativity as they
plan for opening day.
But an emptiness
enshrouds this
new beginning.

Within a silent
chamber of my heart,
sadness dwells,
for among my
friends and co-workers,
one is missing. Gone
is her laughter and
our times of sharing.

The senselessness of
her untimely death
clouds my understanding
and I question,
*Why was one so dedicated
to nurturing others silenced
in the prime of her life?*

*Why in the spring,
when new life was
budding, did death
come unbidden?*

I strain to hear your
answers, but instead
only the echoes of my
questions resound
within my mind.

I realize that the peace
I seek can only be found
in acceptance and trust.

Father, you know the
intricate design of life
and you are sovereign.
What you do not will,
you allow for reasons

unknown to man. Help
me to trust your wisdom.

Always, I will cherish
her memory. It will
warm my heart when
I miss her the most,
for I know a part of
her will never die.
Because she touched
others,
   she
      lives
         on.

(Dedicated to the memory of Nadia Nebesny
Mitchner, who lovingly taught for twenty
years.)

Serve one another in love.

Galatians 5:13

rojecting

It's my turn for
duty in the cafeteria
and wouldn't you
know, it's hot dogs.

Already I envision
hundreds of little hands
uplifted, as they wave
tiny packages of
mustard and ketchup,
beckoning me to
come and open the
resistant containers.

The worst part is the
saliva-slick plastic
gnawed by tiny teeth
in an effort to expel
the seasonings within.

Lord, I need your
patience today. Let
me open each package
with a smile and a secret
blessing upon each student.

What's that, Lord?
Take my scissors?
How simple!

But thou, O LORD, art a shield for me; my glory,
and the lifter up of mine head.

Psalm 3:3 KJV

Shine Like Stars

Here I go again, Lord,
stacking up complaints
like papers to grade.

School has barely begun
and already I have the
grumbling down pat,
    lesson plans are due,
    I don't have a break,
    I have recess duty,
    I have a mountain of
    papers to grade,
    my students are talkative,
    they won't listen, they don't
    put their names on their papers,
        on and on
            I murmur
until my complaining comes
tumbling down,

burying me
in a mound of stress.

Why do I insist
on this unhealthy mode
of handling anxiety?
I know that complaining
only reinforces
my anxiousness.

Help me to stop looking
at my day through
dreary-gray glasses.
Instead, cleanse the
lenses of my outlook.

Remind me that I
can take a spiritual
break with you
   anytime,
     anywhere,
within the privacy
of my thoughts.

I can cast my cares upon
you, for you are my shield,
my glory and the lifter of
my head.

"Martha, Martha," the Lord answered, "you are worried and upset about many things, but only one thing is needed. Mary has chosen what is better, and it will not be taken away from her."

Luke 10:41

First Things First

Whoever coined the
adage,
  a place for everything
  and everything in its place,
hadn't seen
my classroom.

With the arrival
of each academic
year, I determine
to be more organized.

By October, I am
lost in my network
of clutter.

Rubber bands and
pushpins have

become marbleized
in the cup that
is supposed to
hold my pencils.

Paper clips of
all sizes have
filtered from their
individual boxes
to form a chain of
connecting links.

Volcanic mountains
of ditto books,
    teaching manuals,
        and papers to grade
threaten to spew
over and cover
my shelf with
educational debris.

Papers dropped as
randomly as autumn
leaves accumulate
on top of my desk.
Periodically, I rustle
them into new mounds
as I search for the
one I need.

I intend to be neat,
but teaching requires
every moment.
With that statement,
I realize I have chosen
the most important.

Father, don't let me
forget the importance
of putting things away,
but when time is short,
help me to relax
and keep my priorities
in order.
   Teaching comes first.

I tell you the truth, anyone who will not receive
the kingdom of God like a little child will never
enter it.

Mark 10:15

$\mathscr{K}$indred Spirits

$\mathbf{A}$ vivid blue sky
adorned with
puffball clouds
enhances this
picture-perfect day.

Silver slides
radiate the heat
from a heavenly
spray of sunbeams.

In step, an
empty swing dances
with the
energetic breeze.

Voices of
children at play
hopscotch on the
current of the
March wind.

RECESS
and I'm on duty.
The swing, like an
inviting chariot,
beckons to me
and I cannot resist.

My teacher's eyes
are still on patrol,
as my childlike heart
soars heavenward.

Quickly the
call goes out
to come and see,
and I am surrounded
by my pint-sized playmates.

Joy dances in
their eyes and
the child in me

bonds with the
child in them.
Now they know
we are kindred spirits.
  Why, this teacher is really okay.

Father, thank you
for the richness of
this sweet communion.

*If my people, who are called by my name, will
humble themselves and pray and seek my face and
turn from their wicked ways, then will I hear from
heaven and will forgive their sin and will heal
their land.*

2 Chronicles 7:14

*If the foundations are destroyed, what can the
righteous do?*

Psalm 11:3 RSV

The Kaleidoscope

One nation under God . . ."
Lord, I know that is
how it began, but this
country no longer
turns to you for counsel.

Man in his prideful
intelligence seeks to
protect his freedom
and does away with
the freedoms that this
nation was founded upon.

Like the tinted pieces
of a kaleidoscope falling
into new alignment,
today's changing society
continually evolves into
new patterns. Daily I
must contend with
society's imprint
upon my students.

Out of sync with your
rhythm, this generation
lives enslaved by their
fast-paced lifestyles.

Mornings, rushed by
parents arriving home,
or scurrying to work,
produce confusion in
the lives of my students.

Sleepy and unkempt,
students stumble
toward their desks
each morning
with growling stomachs,
    no time for breakfast.

Stressed-out adults
form dysfunctional families

and produce
emotionally starved children.

The proverb, "spare
the rod and spoil the child,"
has become a reality.

Manners are passé and
rudeness is the norm.
The meaning of respect
remains dormant
in the dictionary.

Values lack meaning
when they are not
based on godly principles.

Sometimes it
overwhelms me.
They are all so needy.

Still, you have called
me to teach,
to feed your sheep.
How I long to mend
their broken spirits
and bring your peace
to their
storm-tossed lives.

Energize me
as I seek to
shepherd the flock
you have placed
within my class.

Enable me as
I attempt this
monumental task.

Empower me with
your wisdom as I
devote myself to
teaching through the
changes in society.

Is there anything of which one can say, "Look! This is something new"? It was here already, long ago; it was here before our time.

Ecclesiastes 1:10

A Stabilizing Influence

Thematic instruction
phonics   whole-language
cooperative learning   individualized instruction
hands-on   daily drill
discovery method

Like a bicycle wheel,
the cycle in education
turns continually,
and teachers, as
well as students,
get caught between
the spokes.

Father, restore to us
our lost confidence.
Cause us to not

always question our
teaching ability.

Release in us the
courage to stand
firm and use the
methods that we
have found to work.

Rescue us from
feeling like we
are in bondage
to the textbook.

Remind us that
we are to be
the hub that
secures the wheel
and gives balance
to the trends in
education.

If someone forces you to go one mile, go with him two miles.

Matthew 5:41

For I am the LORD, your God, who takes hold of your right hand and says to you, Do not fear; I will help you.

Isaiah 41:13

ome Days . . .

Some
days
it
seems
easy,
some
days
it
seems
too
long,
going
the
extra
mile.

Lord, you set the
example and you
command us in
your Word.

But I am still
reluctant, for my
energy is depleted
by an overly
taxing schedule.

Work overload
frustrates me as
I surrender my
free moments and
give up the pursuit
of my own interests.

Like an apple
quickly consumed
bite by bite,
my time
is snatched away
minute by minute
by someone else's agenda.

Infinite demands
cause the
seed of resentment
to germinate

and the weed of stress
begins to grow.

Questions surface,
How will I manage?
How will I get through
this year, this week, or
even today?

Immediately you respond,
speaking within my mind,
promising,
I WILL HELP YOU.

I wonder,
Will I trust you?
Will I let you,
or am I too engrossed in
my private pity party to
allow you to comfort me?

Lord, when the requests
to go the extra mile
seem multiple,
help me uproot
any shoots of bitterness
and give them to you.
Plant within my heart,
the fruit of your Spirit.

Incite me to obedience,
trusting you to
redeem my time and
renew my fatigued body.
Let me remember that
no matter how long
the extra mile may seem,
   you walked to
   Golgotha for me.

But this precious treasure—this light and power
that now shine within us—is held in a perishable
container, that is, in our weak bodies. Everyone
can see that the glorious power within must be
from God and is not our own.

2 Corinthians 4:7 TLB

A Journal Entry

Just a journal entry,
    charming and cute,
        flattering and rewarding.

"I wanna be a teacher like . . ."

Smiling, I jot a
thank you and
start to lay her
journal aside.

As instantaneously as
flipping a light switch,
understanding illuminates
my mind and I perceive
clearly the magnitude

of her statement:
> *Here is a child*
> *that respects me,*
>> *that wants to be*
>> *just like me.*
>> *She has chosen*
>> *to model her life*
>> *after me.*

Father, help me to live
so that I reflect
your light and power
in my daily life.

Grant my students
vision to recognize
that I have this
precious treasure.

As I seek to
model my life
after you,
may they too,
seek to be imitators
of Christ Jesus.

Help me to be
worthy of your
high calling.

Therefore, there is now no condemnation for those who are in Christ Jesus, because through Christ Jesus the law of the Spirit of life set me free from the law of sin and death.

Romans 8:1–2

A Complicated Task

It is my least
favorite time,
the end of a
grading period.

Acting as judge
and jury, I transfer
averages from my
gradebook to minute
squares on pink
report cards.

It is true that my
students have earned
the grades entered in
my book. But I am
constantly questioning,

Why does Ryan
have that low grade?
Didn't he feel well
that day? How unlike
Suzie to have a ninety-
seven. Did she copy
from a neighbor's paper?
Always, I seek
to be fair.

The borderline grades
pose an even greater
problem,
> *Have my students*
> *done their best; or*
> *could they do even*
> *better?*

Father, you are the
perfect judge, but
I wonder if it's
like this for you.
Do you dislike
having to pronounce
judgment?

I think it must be
so, for you sent
your Son to live,

die, and be resurrected
for us.

And when we
accept him
as our Lord
and Savior,
then, and only
then, do we
escape a failing
grade and receive
eternal life.

For where you have envy and selfish ambition,
there you find disorder and every evil practice.
                                                    James 3:16

A $\mathscr{P}$erplexing Question

 A cloud of anxiety
envelops the school
as the week of
testing arrives.

Teachers fill in bubbles,
or strive to apply
computer labels in
straight alignment.
Important student data
must be relayed to
the test processors.

Pencil sharpeners
grind incessantly
as students make
sure that they have
one for use and
one for a spare.

Like a stuck phonograph needle,
teachers have reiterated daily,
   Get a good night's sleep.

Some teachers serve
a nutritious snack
in an effort to squelch
lack of concentration
due to hunger pangs.
All effort must be
made to eliminate
low test scores.

After trips to the restroom
and drinking fountains,
signs of
   "DO NOT DISTURB"
are posted on every door.
Interruptions must not occur.

In the past, I've
had students
burst into tears
because they didn't
know the answers.

More than once I have
walked away from a
test review meeting,
feeling like a failure.

Then I'd remember,
test scores are contingent
upon many variables,
and I'd go easy on my
damaged self-esteem.

Father, why is testing
so important?
    Do we need it?
        Do the positive benefits
        outweigh the negative?

I have often heard
rumors about schools
where teachers teach the
test, or even help their
students. If testing causes
dishonesty can it be good?

Do we test to find out
if students are comprehending
the material being taught,
or is it to find out where
schools rank?

Has that rank become
the yardstick that schools
use to measure their success?
Is it valid?

Help officials in charge
of education to clearly
perceive this issue.
Cause them to rethink
the *why* of testing,
guide them with
your wisdom.

$\mathcal{M}$y Treasures to Remember

A victorious moment in my teaching

A difficult moment in my teaching

A special moment in my teaching

Part Two

Jewels of Promise

"They shall be mine," says the Lord of Hosts, "in that day when I make up my jewels."

Malachi 3:17 TLB

*How wonderful it is to be able to say the right thing
at the right time!*

Proverbs 15:23 TLB

The Unexpected

Small hands clutch
autumn leaves gathered
on our nature walk.

It is our art and
science lessons rolled
into one, and the
children are excited.

At station one
I gingerly show
them how to
flatten their leaves
to make a rubbing.

Sundry shades of
crimson, bittersweet
squash-yellow and
even a few black
prints begin to appear.

Moving on to station
two, I demonstrate how
to do a watercolor
wash over their rubbings.
They are thrilled to get
to use the paintbrushes.

Intent upon their
work, all is quiet
until one little guy
looks up at me
and says, "This is
more fun than having
my GI Joe with me
all day!"

Outwardly, I chuckle.
Inwardly, my heart sings.
I've just been paid a
high compliment.

Lord, thank you
for this child who
made my day!

*May God who gives patience, steadiness, and
encouragement help you to live in complete harmony with each other—each with the attitude of
Christ toward the other.*

Romans 15:5 TLB

The Waiting Game

The hum of the clock
is the only thing that
can be heard as we
silently wait. Seconds
stretch into infinity.

The children are
watching me as I
bite my lip to keep
from saying something
I'll regret. I refrain
from going to help.
He has to learn.

How many more
minutes will pass
until this student
has gotten his book

out and found his
page so we can
begin reading?
If it isn't soon,
I will have to
go on with
the lesson.

Inwardly I fume
at what seems
to be selfishness
on his part.
He wastes our time
as well as his own.

I have sought
to speed him up,
but to no avail.
Our battles have
been intense.

Father, you in
your wisdom
have shown me
the futility of it all.

Now, I realize that
the only person
I can change is
myself. So I am

endeavoring to be
more tolerant and
accepting of those
who have a different
rhythm than my own.
*I know I always
rush through things.*

Forgive my fretting
and thank you for
granting me wisdom
on how to manage
this stressful situation.

Father, enable me
to become the person
you want me to be.
Shower me with your
patience equipping me to
attend this child with
a Christ-like attitude.

*For when the way is rough, your patience has a
chance to grow.*

James 1:3 TLB

*If you want to know what God wants you to do, ask
him, and he will gladly tell you, for he is always
ready to give a bountiful supply of wisdom to all
who ask him; he will not resent it.*

James 1:5 TLB

A Chance to Grow

Father, this child
bounces around
my room like a
rubber ball,
. . . pong . . . to the
drinking fountain . . . pong . . .
to borrow a pencil . . . pong . . . to the trash can
. . . pong . . . to his seat . . . pong . . .
the cycle begins again.

I've used every method
known to my profession
to get him to cooperate:
counseling,

contracts,
        discipline,
but to no avail. I am
at my wit's end.

Bestow your patience
upon me.

Bless me with your
creativity as I seek to
provide more hands-on
stimuli.
        I know that sitting in
        a chair all day is alien
        to a small child's nature.

Bring into focus
your solution for
managing this child.

An anxious heart weighs a man down, but a kind word cheers him up.

Proverbs 12:25

The Endearment

It was my first
day back after a
bout with the flu.

I weeded my way
through a pile of
notes and papers
trying to acclimate
myself to where
the sub had left off.

Just as I began
to teach, I heard
the words,
> *"I sure did
> miss you."*
Turning to see
who had spoken,
I was surprised.

It was not one of
my diligent students,
but one with whom
I am often at odds.

Looking into his
huge brown eyes,
I knew he meant it,
and I thanked him.

Like the antibiotic
that cured my illness,
his kind words destroyed
the irritating germs
of frustration that
I had been experiencing.

At last, I began to
relax. I would get
reoriented and soon
my teaching would
flow smoothly.
I reminded myself
that the first day
back is always
the hardest.

Suddenly the trials
of the morning seemed

small in comparison
to the endearment
I had been given.
I do make a difference.

I had been absent
and I was missed.

*But the LORD says, "Do not cling to events of the
past or dwell on what happened long ago."*
Isaiah 43:18 GNB

The Difficult Move

Father, this new student
has been here almost
three weeks and the
other children have gone
out of their way to make
him feel welcome.

Still he refuses to join
in, and at lunch, he insists
on having his "own space."
In a sea of playful
bodies, he remains a
solitary figure at recess.

During P. E. he balks
at participating on a
team. Pushed to the
point of exasperation

myself, I try talking
with him.

I explain that we
love him and want
him to be a part
of our class.

Crying softly,
he raises his
tear-streaked face
toward me and
speaks,
    "But I don't like any
    of you. I want
    my old school back."

Now, I understand.

By not accepting us,
he thinks he can go
back to his old friends.

Gently, I tell him
the hard truth, that
he can't go back, that
he can only go ahead.

In a little while he
joins us and I know

with time, he will
be okay.

Father, embrace this
student and others
like him who have
to shed the cocoon
of the familiar and
try their wings in
unknown territory.

Travel with them and
help them to grow
through the changes
in their lives.

Plant within them
a sense of adventure
and the ability to
make new friends.

For he will give his angels charge of you to guard you in all your ways. On their hands they will bear you up, lest you dash your foot against a stone.
Psalm 91:11-12 RSV

Entering into Emptiness

Taped inside lunch boxes,
hidden in school desks,
dangling from chains,
    KEYS,
no welcome smiles
to greet the latchkey
kids of today.

Anxiousness tugs
at their senses
as they masquerade
in bravery, unlocking
doors and entering
into emptiness.

Ice or snow,
resulting in early

school dismissal,
intensifies their problems
and requires them
to be alone
most of the day.

A list of "don'ts"
itemized by apprehensive
parents is attached to the
refrigerator. Adherence
to the rules will bring
promised surprises.

Like a thief, anxiety
robs today's children
of their carefree childhood.

Father, only you possess
the answer to this
modern-day problem.

> Prevail upon schools
> to be a part of the solution.

> Provide parents with your
> wisdom for their child's welfare.

> Protect these little ones
> within your arms and
> calm their fears.

*Let there be complete silence. . . . Not a single word
from any of you until I tell you . . .*
                                        Joshua 6:10 TLB

The *N*oisemakers

With a *bing, bing, bing*
and a *pi-pi-pitta,* the noise-
makers have arrived. My
day begins in an explosion
of auditory utterances.

Father, what is it
with boys and sounds?
Did you equip them
with larynxes designed to
mimic every tone created?

I'll agree that they may
grow up and make
valuable contributions
to society, but for today,
silence would be golden.
Even a momentary hush

would help me regain
my sanity.

How do I quiet the
continual barrage of
noise? It seems an
impossible task.

I've told them to
turn off their noise-
makers, shut off
their motors, and
park their cars. I've
threatened, and I've
even tried ignoring
them, but to no avail.

This situation must
be resolved, for there
are students who need
the stillness to concentrate.

If I have overlooked the
obvious, please reveal to
me your solution for this
harmless but annoying
problem,
    *and Father, please
    make it soon.*

*For he has not despised or disdained the suffering
of the afflicted one; he has not hidden his face from
him but has listened to his cry for help.*
Psalm 22:24

Arise, cry out . . . for the lives of your children.
Lamentations 2:19

The Oppressed

Desiring to rescue
students with battered
lives and splintered
personalities, we teachers
experience frustration
when we report abuse
and meet with resistance.

Agencies set up to
assist, often make
matters worse. Poorly
thought-out strategies
for intervention cause
smoldering situations to
explode in violence.

Many times we ask
ourselves,
> *Have we made matters*
> *worse by reporting our*
> *suspicions?*

> *Have we helped at all?*

Filled with anxiety
over a problem in
which we have no
control, we spend our
nights tossing restlessly.

We are sickened in
the pit of our stomachs
as our minds replay the
tales of torment.

The next day, we search
through weary eyes for
evidence that the abuse
has happened again.

Fear grips us when a
reported family moves away.
Years later we find
ourselves wondering,
> *What ever happened*
> *to that tortured child?*

Did she grow to adulthood?
Did someone save her from
her nightmarish existence?

Lord, it is hard for me
to understand. My heart
breaks to see the innocent
suffer. I know it grieves
you too. It is *not* your will.

This is an evil and perverted
generation that fills its mind
with violence and pornography,
while selling its soul for
alcohol and drugs.

Still you wait patiently for
these sin-sick lives to turn
to you and be healed.

I do not question your
wisdom, for my vision
is limited. I only see a
part of the whole of life.

But I do ask that you
spur teachers to act
as your arms, enfolding
these precious children.

Guide us daily as our
lives entwine with
these wounded spirits.
Open the channels,
allowing us to rescue
these victims of oppression.

For the LORD sees not as man sees; man looks on
the outward appearance, but the LORD looks on the
heart.

1 Samuel 16:7 RSV

Do not store up riches for yourselves here on earth,
where moths and rust destroy, and robbers break in
and steal. Instead, store up riches for yourselves in
heaven, where moths and rust cannot destroy, and
robbers cannot break in and steal. For your heart
will always be where your riches are.

Matthew 6:19–21 GNB

The *R*ight Reasons

Flashing like neon signs,
"brand names"
silently voice
my students' cries
for acceptance.

Fluorescent shoelaces
dangling from the
latest foot attire,
glow beneath my
students' desks.

Jeans and shirts
bearing the logos
of the latest trends
make a fashion
statement of who
is "in" and who is not.

Father, what have
we done to our children?
Did the quest to
accumulate "things"
become the battle cry
of a nation recovering
from the Depression era?

Is greed like ink,
spilling over and
blotting from sight
the intrinsic value
of man?

The truth is
we have become
a nation focused
only on
extrinsic values.

Wake up the people
within this land.

Save us from this idolatry.
Give us your vision.

Speak to the hearts
of parents and teachers.
Together let us
start to reshape
the value system
of this land.

Stir the hearts of
parents causing them
to refuse to work
two jobs, or overtime
to provide the
"top of the line"
for demanding children.
By this act, may their
lives proclaim,
relationships are more
important than things.

I know you do
not deny your
children nice things.
Having some fashionable
items is fun and nurtures
our self-concept,
but when they become
our god, it grieves you.

May we as teachers
set the example.
*We don't have to have
a fashion stamp on
everything we wear.*

Help us keep our
perspective and
value *hearts*
instead of *things*.
Let our desire
for acceptance be
for the right reasons.

For I will restore health unto thee, and I will heal
thee of thy wounds, saith the LORD.
Jeremiah 30:17 KJV

The *E*pidemic

The flu season
is upon us, and
I feel like I'm
running an infirmary.

Watering eyes
peer out
at me from
pale, listless faces.

Between coughs,
I have been sending
students home.

Passing out papers,
I pause at the desk
of one little brunette.
She looks up at me
through feverish eyes,

and I know the
invading virus has
claimed another victim.

Without hesitation,
I write her a pass
and send her to the
nurse.

Returning shortly,
she announces that her
temperature is 1-0-8.
Amused, I know she
means 100.8.

Quickly we gather
her things and I wish
her a speedy recovery.
I know I will not
see her for a week.

Only a handful
of students remain,
and they don't feel
well enough to
concentrate. I will
have to change my
lesson plans.

Father, heal these
students who are ill.
Fill their caretakers
with compassion
and see that they
get medical attention
if needed.

And for me,
    help me to
        readjust,
            relax,
                and review.

You have taught the little children to praise you perfectly.

Psalm 8:2 TLB

The Perfect Answer

Daily I watch
students who suffer
because their lives
are steeped in chaos
brought on by alcohol
and drug abuse.

Providing volumes of
information, I teach
recognition of good drugs
and bad drugs.

With a passion, I present
the consequences
of addiction, hoping it
will serve as a deterrent.

How I long to see
the bonds broken

and those who are
already entrapped,
set free.

Father, this afternoon
I was wrapping up my
presentation, explaining
to my students where
help could be obtained,
when I saw the small
hand waving.

Calling on the
tiny redhead,
she proclaimed,
    "Why, you could
    tell Jesus. I love
    Jesus more than
    anything and he
    will help us."

A hush fell upon
our class as wisdom
emanated from the
mouth of a babe.

Recovering from
the unexpected,
I assured her that
she was right. I

marveled that she
had recognized
a truth that many
adults never grasp.

Father, I know that
you use various agencies
to bring healing to lives,
but let me take her
statement to heart and
seek your direction before
I endeavor to guide
those in need of counsel.

Father, bless this child
for her perfect praise
and bring healing to
her family.

He will never let me stumble, slip or fall. For he is
always watching, never sleeping. Jehovah himself is
caring for you! He is your defender. He protects
you day and night. He keeps you from all evil, and
preserves your life. He keeps his eye upon you as
you come and go, and always guards you.

Psalm 121:3–8 TLB

The *A*wesome Responsibility

An array of bus notes
hastily written on
remnants of paper,
speckle my door casing,
rerouting my students to
different locations nightly.

Monday and Tuesday
Chris is to come home.
On Wednesday and
Thursday, he is to ride
bus nine to grandma's.
On Friday, his dad will
pick him up.

It is no wonder that
each afternoon at 3:05,
Allison starts to cry,
confused over which
bus to ride. Every
other night she travels
to a different sitter,
yet her mom expects
her to remember.

Checking my
master sheet,
I wonder if her
mom remembers.
I'd be lost
without my list.

My day ends
in a frenzy
when a parent calls
prior to dismissal
and I fail to get the
message, or worse yet,
in the busyness of
day's end, I overlook
the note and a child
gets on the wrong bus.

Frantic phone
calls go out,

and prayers go up,
with the hope
that interception
can take place.

Only when I know
that my student has
arrived safely in the
arms of family, do I
breathe freely again.

Father, guide these
children who have
been given such an
awesome responsibility.
Lead them through
the maze of yellow buses,
bringing today's number
to their minds. Deliver them
safely to their destinations.

Prompt me to
continually check my list
against incoming notes
and make me efficient
in dispensing students
on their prescribed
journey for each day.

But the Lord said ". . . you are so upset over all these details! There is really only one thing worth being concerned about."

Luke 10:41–42 TLB

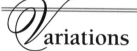

Variations

Confetti-like paper
clippings and pencils
strewn here and there
lay amidst today's
work and textbooks
on the floor.

The comic strip
character Pig Pen
has nothing on
this child.

Several times a day
I stop and remind
him to clean up his
floor and to quit
snipping paper.

He's fascinated
with his scissors.

But we have to go
deeper and clean
his desk, for its
gaping mouth
is bulging with
  trash,
      incomplete work,
        an extra shirt,
          toys, and part of
            his uneaten lunch.

It is the last
grading period
of the year and
all my techniques
for teaching
organization have
failed with him.

  Some days, I can't
  stand it! I can't
  function in clutter.

But today as my
focus was drawn to
his messy floor, I
looked up until my
eyes rested on his face.

His features exuded
happiness and contentment
as he worked on
his lesson, oblivious
to the mess beneath
his feet.

Could it be that
I am too concerned
with neatness?
    Isn't an inward
    peace what most
    of us desire?
        Have I been
        looking down
        when I should
        have been
        looking up?

Lord, I'll continue to
try to help him with
this problem, for I
know you are a God
of order. But may I
be mindful that disorder
precedes creation, and
this mess may be
his creativity oozing
out all over my floor.

May it be foremost
in my mind that you
made many variations
of your children and
you love us all.
 *Why, he doesn't have
to be just like me.*

Be merciful, just as your Father is merciful.
Luke 6:36

A Glimpse of Your Love

It was a hot, sweltering afternoon when it happened. Without a moment's hesitation, I took this child into the hall and began my lecture.

> *"How could you*
> *have done this?*
> *This is so unlike*
> *you. How cruel*
> *you have been.*
> *Do you know*
> *what you deserve?*
> *I'm going to . . ."*

But then you stopped me. Suddenly, in my

mind's eye, I became
that child and you my
teacher.

I remembered when I
failed you. I deserved
to be lectured, to be
disciplined.

I felt your eyes of
disappointment upon
my soul, and I was
sorry for the wrong
I had done.

Unlike me, you had
no anger, only forgiveness
and a reminder to do better.

A split second,
    frozen in eternity,
        a glimpse of your love,
            and I showed mercy.

        "I love you and I expect
        better from you. I'm
        going to forget this incident
        ever happened. Go back to
        your seat and learn from
        this experience."

Father, thank you
for this revelation,
reminding me of
the grace you have
bestowed upon me.

Give, and it will be given to you. A good measure,
pressed down, shaken together and running over,
will be poured into your lap. For with the measure
you use, it will be measured to you.
Luke 6:38

ictory Day

At first they wanted
to laugh, to poke fun
at this little gal every
time she made an "F."

But I explained to
them that they needed
to be thinking of ways
to help her succeed.

So it was in the weeks
ahead that I would often
see them drilling her on
math facts or vocabulary.

One by one, they took
their turns helping her

trace her spelling words
in the sand.

PEER TUTORING,
 a professional tag for
  students caring enough
   to give of themselves
    and help a classmate learn.

Today, it happened.
We were playing
spelling baseball
when this "little gal"
correctly spelled
her word.

Spontaneously, the
whole class cheered.

With a smile that
stretched from
ear to ear, she
ran on to base.

It was a prize-
winning day,
a reaping of rewards.

For in reaching out
to help another, each

student experienced a
victory in his heart.

Father, thank you
for these "precious jewels"
and their caring hearts.

$\mathscr{M}$y Treasures to Remember

An endearment that I received from a student

My special concerns for my students

Funny things that my students have said

PART THREE

A Treasury of Moments

The LORD shall open unto thee his good treasure.
Deuteronomy 28:12 KJV

*And you show that you are a letter from Christ . . .
written not with ink, but with the Spirit of the living God, not on tablets of stone, but on tablets of
human hearts.*

2 Corinthians 3:3 RSV

*And now these three remain: faith, hope and love.
But the greatest of these is love.*

1 Corinthians 13:13

A *New* Beginning

Leaves spiral downward
ushering in fall as teachers
and staff gather anew.

Arriving with hopes
rekindled and energies
restored, they are
reluctant to bid
farewell to their
season of rest.

Sighs of, "Summer
sure went fast!"
breeze in and out
of conversations.

An undercurrent of
excitement pulsates
among the staff as
each one anticipates and
hopes for a good year.

Like the blank pages
of a new plan book,
the academic year lies
before us, unwritten.

Supply us with
your wisdom as
we write upon
the pages of
these young lives.

Strengthen our faith,
helping us to believe
that we can and do
make a difference.
Allot to us the ability to
teach the whole person.

Spark hope within
us for our students,
causing it to flame
brightly, turning on
the light of knowledge

within these young
minds.

And now, Father,
let the year begin.

Fill its pages with
faith, hope and love.

Remind us often
that love writes
on hearts in
permanent ink.

You shall be a crown of beauty in the hand of the
LORD, and a royal diadem in the hand of your God.
Isaiah 62:3 RSV

Charm is deceptive, and beauty is fleeting.
Proverbs 31:30

*F*orever Bound

The combs have been
delivered and we have
been bidden. The moment
is upon us. Picture-taking
day has arrived.

Hurriedly I progress
down my line of students
making sure they are
in a state of perfection.

Cowlicks determined
to do their own thing
resist my efforts to
flatten them.

Baby-fine hair secured
with spray, defies the
comb's teeth, making
its passage an impossibility.

A neglected mass of
tangles, complete with
bed lint, requires extra
moments.
    I hope it's
    just lint.

At last, with collars
straightened and bows tied,
we proceed to the library
for our group picture.

Students arranged in
stairstep heights, form
three rows of order. I
take my appointed place
among them.

With a snap of the
shutter we are immortalized,
forever bound together
as a class.

Quickly, the photographer
hands me the polaroid shot

for identification purposes.
Glancing at my image,
truth hurts and I wish I had
taken my summer dieting
program more seriously.

Advancing to station two,
I scan the ranks, assuring
that my students are ready
for their individual photos.
Bulbs flash rapidly as two
photographers make haste.

Silently, I stand by as
toothless grins appear
on freshly scrubbed
faces,
    Cherubs in disguise.

Amused, I watch as
a few students curl
lips under teeth, plastering
on the fixed smile that
they think is desired.

Returning to the classroom,
our day of ordinariness
stretches before us. We
are momentarily let down
that the special event has

come and gone so quickly.
Suddenly a student calls
out, "When will we get
our pictures back?"

Immediately our equilibrium
is restored. Now, we have
something to look forward to.

The righteous will flourish like a palm tree, they will grow like a cedar of Lebanon. . . . They will still bear fruit in old age, they will stay fresh and green.

Psalm 92:12, 14

You shall give due honor and respect to the elderly, in the fear of God.

Leviticus 19:32 *TLB*

A *Day* of Honor

Ultramodern grandparents
with fadeless crowns
and bodies that testify
of healthy diets and
daily workouts
    intermingle with
bald heads bobbing
and coiffures in
shades of silver.
Rounded torsos reveal
that these grandparents
do not resist growing old.

Small hands clasp those
weathered by time,
pulling them along,
escorting them to their
classrooms. Pride is
etched upon each face.
It is a special day, our
time to honor grandparents.

My classroom buzzes
with chatter as students
interview their special
guests,
> *Where did you*
> *go to school?*
> *How did you*
> *get there?*
> *What did you*
> *eat for lunch?*
> *What games did*
> *you play at recess?*

Our attention is riveted
on the tellers of tales
and their stories delight us.

In this unique moment
of sharing, the hours

spent in preparation for
this day seem minute.
I'm glad we have
paused to listen, to
revere those we cherish.

Father, thank you for
this blending of education,
past and present, this
touching of hearts,
spanning the generations.

For you have heard my vows, O God; you have
given me the heritage of those who fear your name.
Psalm 61:5

Our Heritage

Multicolor trees
whisper of ages past,
as apples scent the
air and children get
their first taste of
homemade cider
from a press.

Small hands fluff
the fur of dried
animal skins as
frontier men in
authentic costumes
tell tall tales.

As melodiously as
the swishing of the
autumn leaves, a
folksinger displays

her mountain instruments
and teaches songs
of a bygone era.

Spellbound, students
watch woodcarvers
chip away, releasing
replicas of times past.

Basket weavers
delicately fuse
yesterday with today,
as they explain the
usage of their craft.

Children gathered at
the potter's wheel
watch creation take
form. Vessels of
the pioneer era
begin to take shape,
reminding us that
like them, we too
are unique.

Students scrunch
puffs of wool
as ladies in pioneer
dress turn spinning

wheels and weave
stories as rich as
their thread.

It is an educational
journey into our past,
a hands-on, fun way
to learn, our school's
pioneer day.

It was different,
this life of our
forefathers, and as
an adult, I yearn
for a time that was
slower paced,
    for work that wearied
    the body instead of the
    mind,
        for a time when society's
        energies were spent on survival,
        instead of concocting evil.

Was it a better time,
or just different?
No matter, the thread
of change weaves its
way inevitably forward
through the fabric of
this nation.

Father, thank you for
the richness of our
heritage. Motivate these
children to grab hold
of the thread from
whence our forefathers
came and with your
wisdom, weave the
fabric of our future.

He holds victory in store for the upright, he is a shield to those whose walk is blameless, for he guards the course of the just and protects the way of his faithful ones.

Proverbs 2:7–8

Champions

Driving past our high school, I see the sign placed proudly by the road, declaring to all who pass by,
STATE FOOTBALL
CHAMPS
and I remember . . .
the wide eyes of the elementary children as they were bussed to the high school for the ultimate in pep sessions.

I'll never forget the thrill as the spark of

excitement ignited
and pride in our school
flamed brightly
throughout the community.

The possibility of a
State Championship
had whet the
desire for fame,
and fans multiplied
as our team brought home
trophy after trophy.

We had given them
a spectacular send-off
with a motorcade that
seemed to stretch into
infinity.

In my mind, I can still
see our team running
onto the field at the
state finals, with
fans screaming wildly
and cheerleaders
    springing here,
springing there.

But what a glorious
moment it was when

in a pre-game silence,
our team knelt in prayer,
surrendering the game
to you—a powerful testimony
to a packed stadium.

They won the championship,
but at the celebration,
they scored another
touchdown in the heart
of the community when
they placed the
revered game ball
on the lap of a classmate,
a young woman
paralyzed since grade school.

Her determination
had shown them
that she was
a true champion
in this game of life.

Father, what wonderful
heroes these young men
were to their peers,
our elementary students,
and the community.

Bless them for their
faithfulness to you
and their unselfish act
of giving away a
prized possession.

Go with them through
life and may they always
be winners for you.

How can light live with darkness? And what harmony can there be between Christ and the devil?
                              2 Corinthians 6:14–15 TLB

But I am frightened, fearing that in some way you will be led away from your pure and simple devotion to our Lord, just as Eve was deceived by Satan in the Garden of Eden. You seem so gullible: you believe whatever anyone tells you.
                              2 Corinthians 11:3–4 TLB

The *H*alloween Dilemma

Smiling jack-o-lanterns
and tissue ghosts
embodied with lollipops
fill my primary classroom
with the spookiness
of Halloween.

Innocent participation
in an established holiday,
but decorations are
becoming more grotesque.

Horror is "in" and evil
abounds on Halloween night.

Movie producers
struggle to top last
season's spine-chiller.
Minds are poisoned
by the occult.

Father, cause teachers
throughout this nation
to stop and reevaluate
this holiday.
Do we continue
to participate in
a holiday that
once was pagan?

Have we deluded
ourselves into thinking
of it as harmless?

Do we redirect it,
creating our own
celebration of autumn?

Guide us as we seek
your direction, turning to
your Word for truth, and
trusting you for discernment.

Give thanks to the Lord, call on his name; make known among the nations what he has done.

Psalm 105:1

The Most Important Truth

Make-believe Indians wearing fawn-colored vests fashioned from grocery sacks gather outside a tepee with a mock blaze.

Heads adorned with construction paper feathers attached to wallpaper headbands are bent over tubs of corn. Feverishly, students work with rocks in hand, grinding corn.

Across the room, trunks made of shoeboxes and

packed with paper replicas
of the Pilgrim's possessions,
rest on desks aligned in
two rows.

White posterboard sails
dangle from the ceiling
above the pretend Mayflower.

On board, smiles shine
from under white muslin
caps and black top hats.
How angelic my students
look in their Pilgrim garb.

November, the season
of thankfulness, of learning
and role playing. How I
love teaching about our
founding fathers.

But don't let me get
so caught up in the
activities that I forget
to teach the most
fundamental truth
of the whole story.
    The Pilgrims were on
    a journey to find a land

where they could worship
you in freedom.

Father, commission
me to convey the value
of this legacy. Spark
within my students
the desire to uphold
this precious freedom.
Then my heart
will be truly filled
with thanksgiving.

I will be your God through all your lifetime, yes,
even when your hair is white with age. I made you
and I will care for you.

Isaiah 46:4 TLB

A Christmas Visit

Patients, aided by
walkers and wheelchairs,
inch their way to
the dining room.
Eagerly they await the
arrival of our students.

An elderly gentleman
in a Santa suit is
posted by the door.

Patting his cotton beard,
he greets our busload
of children with a
hearty "Ho-Ho!"
as they rush in on
a current of cold
December air.

Briefed on what
to expect, the children
quietly take in the
wheelchairs and crutches.
Looks of apprehension
appear on small faces
as they hear the cries of
patients lost in memory.

Decked out in holiday
finery, our carolers
file into formation
and raise their angelic
voices in song.

Memories of Christmases
past stir within the hearts
of the residents and many
join in the singing.

After the program,
boys and girls mingle
with patients, presenting
them with handmade
ornaments.

Anxieties forgotten,
communion flows easily
between the generations.

Misty-eyed, I watch a
shriveled lady in a wheelchair
plant a kiss
on the cheek of a
child starved for love.

Like the Christmas Star,
the moment shone forth
with the true meaning
of Christmas,
   the giving of one's self.

Father, thank you
for a school
that allows us to
reach out to mankind
and teach students
more than academics.

He changes times and seasons.

Daniel 2:21

Melting the Winter Blahs

Beyond the window,
it is a crystal clear day.
The January sun shines
brightly on the frozen
sculpture of snow
blanketing the ground.

Inside our classroom,
snowmen made of
Styrofoam packing chips
form a silent audience
watching us from
above the chalkboard.

Plastic daffodils form
a cheerful centerpiece for
the red-checkered tablecloth
lying on the floor.

Students wearing sunglasses
and summer caps

munch sandwiches and chips.
A multicolored beach ball
rolls onto our spread,
defying that we are
in the heart of winter.

A January picnic,
where the only ants
in attendance are the
ones in our ant farm.

It is the grand finale of
our unit on food groups.
But even more, it is a
reminder that winter
will pass and summer
will return.

Father, for the merriment
of this moment and for
melting the winter blahs
from our hearts, we
give thee thanks.

For I hate divorce, says the Lord *the God of Israel,*
and covering one's garment with violence, says the
Lord *of hosts. So take heed to yourselves and do*
not be faithless.

Malachi 2:16 RSV

The *Lesson*

I meant it to be a lesson
on Dr. King's quote:
    "I have a dream . . ."

I meant for them to
share their dreams
for righting a wrong
within our nation.

With our chairs in a
circle, we began. The
first student told of a
bus situation. Then the
second child said,
    "I know something
    that's not right and
        it's your mom and

dad getting a divorce.
I have a dream that
my parents will get
back together."

Like a hot potato
it spanned our circle,
as students as broken
as their homes shared
their dreams of Eden.

As I sat silently
watching this drama
unfold, I had the
uncanniest feeling
that I was a therapist
with miniature adults.

But they weren't
adults. They were
children with shattered
dreams,
     and I wept.

Father, heal the homes
within this land. Mend
the hearts of these
little souls, for my
dream is to
     rescue the children.

All the special gifts and powers from God will
someday come to an end, but love goes on forever.
1 Corinthians 13:8 TLB

The Transforming Ingredient

Hearts fashioned of
construction paper
and lace doilies
adorn pocket-folders
bulging with sweet
sentiments.

The children chatter
incessantly in anticipation
of the valentine party.

As the time arrives,
I am spellbound as
I watch my students
become transformed
with tenderness.

Coos of, "Look
what she gave me!" and
"O-o-oh, thank you!"
sail about on wings
of love.

Father, how is it
that this festivity
seems even more
precious than our
Christmas party?

Then, they received a
two-dollar toy that
held their attention
for a few minutes.

Today, these cards
of affection alight
their faces with
tenderness and I
bask in the glow.

Dancing eyes pore
over valentines and
students are reluctant
to lay one down and
move on to another.

Could it be that
hearts are hungry
for love and these
cards are symbolic
of something more
important than a
store-bought gift?

Are they tokens
reminding them
that someone cares?

Father, wrap my
class in this tenderness.

Let the sweetness
of this moment,
    linger,
        linger,
            linger.

Her children arise and call her blessed; her hus-
band also, and he praises her.

Proverbs 31:28

A Mother's Day Surprise

Cinderella feet drag
oversized high heels,
click-clacking along
in fashionable steps.

Wearing Mom's oldest
cast-offs, accented with
garage sale accessories,
our Mother's Day
fashion show begins.

Escorts, sporting
Dad's rejected ties,
old caps, and faded
shirts, hook arms
with our clackers and
propel them down
the fashion runway

to the strains of
classical music.

Acting as emcee,
I attempt to conceal
my amusement, but
as "tee-hees" escape
from surprised moms,
laughter of love
fills my classroom.
> *Dads will feel smug to*
> *have helped us pull off*
> *the surprise of the year.*

Children collapse in
their mom's loving
arms as our show
comes to a close.

Shedding costumes,
students excitedly
gather at the
refreshment table,
eager to honor
their mothers.

Pink punch in
crystal cups
slushes from
side to side

as children carry
teetering vessels
to their guests.

May these mothers
add this priceless
pearl of an event
to their strands
of memories
and wear them
forever close
to their hearts.

And let us not be weary in well doing: for in due
season we shall reap, if we faint not.

Galatians 6:9 KJV

Be gentle and ready to forgive.

Colossians 3:13 TLB

The Debut

Video cameras
polka-dot the
crowd as parents
seek to capture
their child's first
debut on stage.

Excitement runs
rampant among
the ranks. Students
with stage jitters
giggle and wiggle,
as I anxiously
stand behind the
curtain and peer out
at the crowd.

Parents nervously
fidget with the focus
on their cameras as
they chat with their
neighbors in the
audience.

At last the curtain
parts. The big
moment has arrived.

Act one unfolds
without a hitch.
Stars are born.
*Why, they're brilliant. They
all know their lines.*

Like a yo-yo, the
microphone continues
to go up and down
depending on the
height of the speaker.
*I warned them, they're
going to drop it.*

How cute they look
in their costumes,
making dim my memory
of the chaotic practices.

A few, with their
monkey antics
of swinging
on the stair railing,
backstage chattering,
and constant peeking
under the curtain,
had caused me to threaten
to close the show
before it opened.

Always, I questioned
why I put myself
through it.
Today I know.

Joining hands for
the final curtain call,
their faces reflect
success. We have
just made another
golden nugget
to add to our
bank of memories.

For we are God's workmanship, created in Christ Jesus to do good works, which God prepared in advance for us to do.

Ephesians 2:10

You have endorsed my work, declaring from your throne that it is good.

Psalm 9:4 TLB

The Long Awaited Day

Lord, it has arrived,
this long awaited day—
        my last day to teach
        before my retirement.

Many times I've
stood in the silent halls
at the close of day
and felt the specialness
of this place.

Deep within my spirit
I sense that what
happens here,

day in and day out,
is important, that
somehow it touches
tomorrow, maybe
even eternity.

How privileged I am
to have been among
the cast of characters
shaping the future
of our world.

That's it, Lord, all my
personal belongings
are boxed. I am
ready to leave.

Is this the right
thing to do? Will
I regret my decision?

Departing, I am at peace.

This place I worked,
this task I did,
        it was good!

My Treasures
to Remember

A holiday moment that I want to remember

A special event that I treasure

An unexpected moment to treasure